Life Lessons
from the
Cat

Amy Newmark

Chicken Soup for the Soul, LLC
Cos Cob, CT

Chicken Soup for the Soul: Life Lessons from the Cat
Amy Newmark

Published by Chicken Soup for the Soul, LLC www.chickensoup.com

The publisher gratefully acknowledges the many publishers and individuals who granted Chicken Soup for the Soul permission to reprint the cited material.

Front cover and interior photo courtesy of iStockPhoto.com/Andrey Kuzmin (© Andrey_Kuzmin).

Interior photo of Amy Newmark courtesy of Susan Morrow at SwickPix

Cover and Interior by Daniel Zaccari

ISBN: 978-1-61159-061-6

PRINTED IN THE UNITED STATES OF AMERICA
on acid∞free paper

25 24 23 22 21 20   03 04 05 06 07 08 09 10 11

Table of Contents

La Chatte

*I love cats because I love my home and after a
while they become its visible soul.*
~Jean Cocteau

I have a left-handed cat. Her name is La Chatte, and my husband and I acquired her by default three years ago, when I was a new stepmother and was in bending-over-backwards mode towards my husband's children, who live with their mother and stepfather on the other side of town.

In a fit of romantic display, my sixteen-year-old stepson had arrived at his paramour's door on her birthday carrying a fluffy, black kitten. The birthday girl's mother was less than enchanted; one is either a cat person or one is not, and I've found that when it comes to cats, there is no middle ground. Wanting to thwart the possibility of her daughter's attachment, the mother spun my stepson around and pointed him in the direction of his car, kitten in hand.

What happened next was a domino effect: my stepson went back home with the kitten, which he handed into the willing arms of his eight-year-old sister who formed a bond with the ball of fur within seconds. Promptly, their mother arrived on the scene followed by the family's four curious dogs. Barking, jumping and general pandemonium ensued, and it didn't take long for their mother to make an executive decision: there would be no kitten living underneath their roof and that was the end of that.

When the phone rang at our house, my husband spent the following half hour trying to soothe his precious daughter, who sobbed and wailed that all was lost because she couldn't keep the kitten. My husband looked at me with desperate eyes so

I gestured for him to hand me the phone. "Tell me about the kitten," I said, and by the end of the day we were the guardians of an appeased eight-year-old, and the permanent caretakers of a nine-week-old black kitten.

Suffice it to say, La Chatte has changed the dynamic of our home, and we have adjusted our lives to accommodate her. She is large on personality, whimsical and capricious. She is aloof until it doesn't serve her, at which point she'll capitulate. She is primarily an indoor cat, but she likes to dart outside should one of our screen doors fall off the track. She never goes very far; she typically just hangs around on the front porch evading us when we give chase and sauntering back inside when it suits her. Rather than being frustrated, I have cultivated an essential patience and am now in the habit of waiting indefinitely to do her bidding.

The reason I know La Chatte is left-handed is because she uses her left paw to get my attention.

When we are seated at the dinner table, she positions herself on the counter behind me and reaches out with her left paw to tap me on my shoulder. This is her way of saying that she wants to join us for dinner even though she has already been fed. If you were to have asked me four years ago if I'd ever envision myself inviting a cat to dinner, I would have told you the idea was preposterous. Yet I have changed my mind completely and I cave every time she taps me, because the gesture is so endearing.

La Chatte is exceedingly vocal for a cat, having figured out quickly that one well timed meow will spur me to action. "What is it, La Chatte?" I say, springing to her command. She'll meow again for good measure just to make sure she's got me, then lead me to the kitchen where her green food bowl with "The Cat" written in white block letters await — because we couldn't find one written in French.

I am the reclining sort, as in I like to lay prone on

the sofa while watching movies. For years I had the exercise down with a soft pillow and throw blanket strategically appointed, but all that changed when La Chatte moved in because she's the affectionate kind who doesn't take no for an answer. She simply insinuates herself onto my chest and all the king's horses couldn't dissuade her, so I have amended my ways to include her. Now no movie would be worth watching without La Chatte's Zen-like presence on my chest.

I have learned that in order to live harmoniously with a cat, you have to accept their premise: they are mysterious little creatures with whiskers, claws, flexible bodies and searing eyes. They are curious, elusive, independent, and fundamentally beyond the reach of human influence until they decide there is something they want from you. I have learned that sometimes in life it's best to suspend judgment and embrace the entire package, even if you never went in search of it. I have learned all this and more. And now I know that sometimes the virtues of patience, acceptance and unconditional love arrive by default in a warm black bundle that purrs.

~Claire Fullerton

The Marks of a Lasting Love

To bathe a cat takes brute force, perseverance,
courage of conviction—and a cat. The last
ingredient is usually hardest to come by.
~Stephen Baker

I t was Mom's fault. She got the ball rolling with one simple, crazy declaration: "WT needs a bath."

Imagine my surprise. WT had been with us for a full year and had shown no symptoms of being especially grimy. I tried to put up a good fight, for her sake and mine.

"What are you talking about?" I asked. "Cats

clean themselves. Constantly. WT doesn't need a bath."

Mom was insistent. "It's been a year. She needs a bath."

It's not that I had any objection to having a clean cat; it was just that I was perfectly happy with WT the way she was. Once more I tried to avert an obvious mistake. "Have you ever tried to give a cat a bath? You know how cats feel about getting wet."

I thought this salvo of good sense would move Mom away from her madness, but she remained adamant. "It's been a year. She needs a bath."

Against such obstinacy the gods themselves strive in vain. Mom's mind was made up: WT had a date with the kitchen sink.

WT had arrived in our lives exactly one year before—on my twenty-first birthday, no less, which made her arrival extra special for me. And over the ensuing twelve months, WT revolutionized our lives.

You see, we had never had a cat before. It had been a long time since we had had any pets. Our most recent pet had been one lonely goldfish with a penchant for jumping out of his bowl; he had made his final flop a couple of years before, and our home had been pet free ever since.

Then our landlord finally relented and gave us the okay to get a cat. So, while I stayed on the couch and celebrated my birthday by watching playoff baseball, Mom and my sister Paula went to the shelter and picked out our new kitty.

Very quickly, our new friend earned the name "Wild Thing," a moniker that was inevitably shortened to her more dignified initials, WT.

WT instantly became the joy of our lives. Everyone doted on her, all day every day: constant petting sessions, countless snapshots to capture her every mood and move, hours of playtime with balls, string, and dozens of toys. Each day of that first year seemed to bring some new delight. A first cat is always a source of endless surprises. You never know what crazy thing kitty will do next—or, as it turned out, what crazy ideas she'll inspire in her human companions.

Like, for instance, the idea that a cat needs a bath.

Crazy or not, that afternoon the three of us herded WT into the kitchen. Before she knew what was happening, we were able to grab WT and get her into the kitchen sink, where Operation Clean Kitty commenced.

The first part of the job went smoothly enough. WT, though profoundly unhappy, favored us with quiet, begrudging, squirmy cooperation. The trouble only truly began when we got the reluctant target of Mom's enforced hygiene routine out of the water.

Paula and I made every effort to dry her off, but—as you can imagine—WT was most interested in beating a hasty retreat. Our hit-and-run attempts with the towels left WT dry enough that I was ready to call it a day.

Again, Mom had other plans. "She's still wet," Mom said, declaring her dissatisfaction. "She needs to be dry."

"She's as dry as she's going to get," I said.

"She's unhappy enough as it is," Paula noted.

"She'll get sick if she's not dry," said Mom.

This, of course, was absurd. "It's almost 90 degrees outside," I said, in mounting exasperation. "She's not going to get sick. The heat will dry her off soon enough."

"She will get sick," Mom insisted. "She needs to be dry."

Again: obstinacy… gods… striving in vain…

And then came the fateful moment. I honestly don't remember who suggested using the hair dryer. In hindsight, an obviously crazy idea. But—as is always the case whenever things really go off the rails—it seemed like a good idea at the time.

So, while my sister got the hair dryer from the bathroom, I kept WT corralled within the kitchen. Soon enough Paula was ready, standing by the kitchen table with the hair dryer plugged in and ready to go. Then I made my move: I grabbed WT and hastened into position, a few feet in front of my sister. I held

WT out in front of me, the same way a person holds a baby who has done terrible things in her diaper.

"Hurry," I advised. "I won't be able to hold her like this very long." Truer words were never spoken.

Paula held up the hair dryer, pointed it at WT, and flipped the power switch.

The results of that fateful action were, literally and figuratively, electric.

The instant the hair dryer roared to life I found myself holding a furry tornado. WT spun around in my hands, like a cartoon Tasmanian devil, in a frenzied and ultimately successful attempt to escape the hair dryer's fury. In the process, her rear claws raked my left forearm, slashing a series of angry-looking gashes from the base of my thumb to halfway down to my elbow. As I howled in shock and pain, WT leapt down to the floor and scrambled away, her revenge already turning bright red along my forearm.

And with that, our "bathe the cat" project came to an abrupt end.

Having done her damage, WT vanished into some faraway hiding place. She got away clean, you might say.

I was not so lucky. Again I spent part of my birthday watching playoff baseball—this time sitting in a chair in the local emergency room.

My wounds, as it turned out, looked impressive but were not particularly dangerous. A bit of professional cleaning, some sterile coating, and a tetanus shot covered my medical needs. All in all, not much damage despite those few seconds of high drama. I would make it home again alive and in one piece.

The funny thing is, I never really blamed WT for the damage she did to me. After all, she had not meant to hurt me; she just wanted to get away from our clumsy attempts at cat grooming. Even if she had scratched me on purpose, she was probably justified. No court in the land would have convicted her.

But something deeper was at work. Later that

night, as I sat on the couch holding up my arm, studying the red streaks that traced the paths of WT's claws, feeling the throbbing ache within those scratches, I knew that I loved WT too much to ever hold such a trivial thing against her. In fact, that incident sealed the deal for me: I was "all in" on being a cat person. A year with WT had shown me the delights that come from letting a cat into your life; a few flesh wounds were a small price to pay for such a blessing.

It has now been ten years since WT passed away. Gus, our family's equally beloved second cat, is also gone and sorely missed. Today, our Maxi holds the office of beloved family cat. These days, I also get to enjoy an extended feline family: a stable of wonderful kitties I know through my cat-sitting clients, plus the numerous cats I've helped prepare for adoption through volunteer work at a local animal shelter—many of whom have gone on to join families and change others' lives in the same way that WT changed my life.

All of the joys that cats have brought to my life began with WT. And those scratches on my arm turned into a set of scars that I have come to cherish. They are not just the physical evidence of a moment when WT literally touched my life; they are also a permanent reminder of WT's legacy, of how she changed my life in so many ways. The scars on my left arm are truly the marks of a lasting love, and I will treasure them until the day I die.

~Stephen Taylor

The Bond of Sisters

Help one another, is part of
the religion of sisterhood.
~Louisa May Alcott

Puma and Kovu were tabby cats with soft gray and black fur that striped and swirled in unique patterns. My sister adopted them both, as they were sisters from the same litter. They lived in an apartment along with my cat, Dakota. Dakota was a beautiful orange male tabby. We decided we'd better get Dakota fixed but it turned out we were too late. Three or four weeks after Dakota's procedure, we realized Puma was getting big around the middle. Another week later we knew she was pregnant.

We got things ready for the kittens and highly anticipated them for weeks.

I woke up in the early hours one morning to Puma meowing softly and nudging my hand. It was time! Puma was very clingy and tried to get as close as she could to me. I had to keep taking her out of my bed and putting her into her pet bed, which she only stayed in when I sat next to it. Eventually the first kitten came.

To watch a birthing process is amazing. How the instincts of the animal kick in and they seem to know exactly what to do. Once the first kitten was out and getting licked by mom, Kovu and Dakota were right there, curious as to what was going on. I was scared they would hurt the kittens, so I shut them in my sister's room while she slept. When I walked back into my room, Puma was meowing and walked over to the closed door the other two cats were behind. I picked her up and put her back in her bed as well as the kitten she had in the middle of the room; however, she wouldn't stay. She kept going back to the closed door, meowing. And as in answering her, Kovu was meowing and reaching her paw under the door.

After several times carrying Puma back to her bed and trying to get her to stay there with her newborn kittens, I gave up with a huff. "Have it your way!" I opened the door and Kovu shot out straight to her sister. They meowed at each other, then Puma led the way into the pet bed and curled up with her kittens, which now totaled three. She touched each one with her nose and looked at Kovu like she was showing them off. Kovu lay down next to the pet bed with her head inside and began to lick one of the kittens. She probably would have crawled right in with Puma, but there wasn't enough room. That is how the rest of the morning went: Puma had four more kittens. She was exhausted and focused on birthing while Kovu stepped in and took over the chore of cleaning each kitten dry.

As the kittens grew, Kovu was in the bed as often as the mother of the litter. She enjoyed keeping them warm and giving each kitten a bath when Mom needed a break. She let the kittens suck on her too though she most likely wasn't producing milk, but neither of the parties seemed to mind. When Puma came back and crawled in, Kovu jumped out. It was a joy seeing the kittens grow up and interact with their mom and aunt.

To this day, I realize just how important it was to Puma to have her sister share that special moment with her. And how important it was to Kovu to be there and help out when her sister couldn't continue doing what she needed to do. They were there for each other. That is a true sister bond that survives through all the years, no matter what.

~Alicia Penrod

Peanut the Pioneer

In a cat's eye, all things belong to cats.
~English Proverb

L earning that my wife was pregnant? Jubilation. Shopping for the lengthy list of necessities at baby stores? Slightly overwhelming. Knowing how those products work? Quite the challenge.

"Honey, not to sound clueless, but I'm completely in the dark about what some of these products do," I told my wife, Joy.

"Don't worry. We will learn it together," she responded happily.

Following our baby shower, I wore out the

asphalt on the driveway carrying in a plethora of boxes of all different sizes with objects that were "foreign" to me inside. In a matter of minutes, we had a mountain of gifts in our living room. How on earth were we going to figure out how to use all these things? Our cat Peanut was eyeing the gifts with some curiosity. Why not let him test some of these products for our soon-to-arrive bundle of joy?

Peanut was an extraordinary feline, and I often wondered if he truly was an invertebrate. He could twist and turn his body in the most peculiar positions that would make even gymnasts and acrobats grimace and gasp. If he was any longer, he could be the reigning champ at *Twister*.

The first item we tore into was a BabyBjorn, (which I finally learned to pronounce after several failed attempts). This thing is designed to hold the baby in front of the parent's torso so that the parent doesn't have to constantly hold the baby. When it was time for Peanut to showcase this item for us, he came scrambling toward us with no idea what we planned. As I picked him up, I whispered into his ear, "Big guy, you are going to be rewarded with many snacks for helping us out."

Trembling a bit with excitement and nerves, I lowered each of his cooperative hind legs into the two openings of the contraption. Once he was in it, he actually looked very tranquil. Joy and I laughed at the sight of Peanut getting an aerial view of our living room while in the BabyBjorn. After I took a few laps around the coffee table with my fluffy friend, we suddenly heard a loud, booming sound coming from him. Indeed, he was purring loudly.

"Unbelievable! He loves it! This thing really must be cozy for babies and… cats. This gift is a keeper," Joy said enthusiastically.

Feeling positive about our first experiment, we decided Peanut should try the play station. From a child's perspective, this was like Disney World! It included colorful shakers that made gentle sounds, a flexible, vivid sun that was as soft as cotton, and realistic farm animal sounds with a simple press of the button.

Shortly after it was assembled, Peanut meandered over to us, as if on cue. He took a seat in the play station and starting jabbing at the plastic sun like a boxer, turning it this way and that. "Unbelievable! Even Rocky Balboa would be proud of Peanut's moves in there," exclaimed Joy.

After the sun was literally down for the count, Peanut swiveled around to his next victim: the shakers. Sniffing each one carefully, he slowly tapped one of the three oddly shaped objects, which produced a high-pitched noise. Unfazed by the sound, he quickly moved over to the other two noisemakers, but seemed bored by them. Without hesitation, he moved to the station that made realistic animal sounds that included a cow, cat, dog, and pig. Since he appeared baffled by what to do, I pressed the cat noise first. His reaction was hilarious! He twisted his head to the side and stared at the speaker intently.

I pressed it again with the same result. As I was going to press it a third time with my eyes focused on Peanut, my finger must've slipped and I pressed the dog, which sounded like a St. Bernard barking. Without hesitation, Peanut's ears went back, and his whole body started to squirm like a worm. Understanding that he was terrified of this sound, I immediately took him out.

Joy and I concluded that Peanut liked moveable objects more than noisy objects. It took a few minutes for him to come back into the room, but when he did, I generously gave him a small handful of meaty treats. All was forgiven.

Shortly after Peanut graciously tried out some of these gifts, my son was born. Fortunately for us, he was not allergic to cats. After passing that hurdle, we wondered how Peanut would react to our son, Colin. It didn't take long for that question to be answered.

On the first night that I gave my son a bottle of

milk using the Boppy, a plush feeding pillow, Peanut wandered over to the rocking chair where I was nervously sitting, suspiciously licking his chops. Peanut touched the Boppy a couple of times and then started licking Colin's feet. I couldn't believe it! He had accepted Colin.

Peanut's involvement didn't end when Colin was a newborn. Several months later, as I put Colin into his crib, I grabbed Peanut, nuzzled him, and plopped him on the Boppy the way he liked it best—inverted. I rocked him and said how much he helped us through this new experience by teaching us to be patient and to understand someone else's feelings through careful observation. As he lay there on the cozy Boppy, I noticed something on his chin. As I brought him over to the light, I detected what I feared. Like butter on bread, pureed green beans were spread all over his fur. It made sense since I didn't clean up the unwanted portion of vegetables from the table. But never did I think Peanut would dive into it. I was wrong. It appears that he wanted to try out everything that we brought home, even the food.

Curiosity might not kill the cat, but it sure makes things a bit messy.

~Austin Tamillo

The Wonder of Birdy

It always gives me a shiver when I see
a cat seeing what I can't see.
~Eleanor Farjeon

From the moment she was born I knew that she was destined for greatness. I can recall holding her in the palm of my hand watching her wiggle and meow, announcing her arrival to the world. I knew that she would be a very independent young feline eager to explore her territory. From the enormous lynx tips on her ears to her silky brown tabby coat, she was everything that I could ask for in a Maine

Coon kitten and I was in love. She was addicted to play and would spend countless hours in hot pursuit of all her favourite toys. She especially loved her cat treats and would wait patiently each day for me to serve her allotted share, always hoping I would spill the bag and she would score extra goodies.

As a very young kitten she would climb to the top of her cat tree and stare out our picture window at the antics of the birds swooping past her vantage point. The sights and sounds she witnessed outside seemed to mesmerize her. It was usually impossible to break her gaze once she focused on an object.

Perhaps it was because of this quirky trait she earned the name Birdy. I delighted in watching her grow into a beautiful young feline with countless energy, eagerly anticipating every event tossed her way. I knew that our Birdy was one special bundle of fur but what I didn't know was that she was destined to save us from a near disaster.

Birdy's special powers were put to the test one

chilly November evening. My husband and I had just started to watch our evening television programs when I noticed Birdy perched on top of our upright piano. Her eyes were locked in a death stare with the wall thermostat. She was a cat with a mission and no amount of coaxing would entice her to relinquish her post. I rattled a bag of her special treats and still she would not move. I thought if anything would catch her attention it would be food, but to no avail.

I sensed that something was very wrong and motioned to my husband Tony to lower the volume so we could hear what captivated our little cat.

"Tony, there is something the matter with Birdy. She won't move. I have tried everything and she won't budge."

"Can you hear the hissing noise?" he exclaimed.

Once we were beside her we saw small flashes of light bursting from the baseboard heater thermostat—the real possibility of fire was not far away.

When my husband removed the cover of the thermostat he discovered electrical arcs sparking from the thermostat cover to the mounting box. We flew into action, shutting off the power and removing the thermostat from the wall. The wooden cedar strips beside the electrical box were severely burned. It terrified us to think that, by the evidence of the burns, the arcing had been happening for quite some time.

The experience left us shaken, overwhelmed and very grateful to our little cat for her perseverance.

"Tony, what if Birdy hadn't heard this? We could have been away." I shuttered. What a marvel our little Birdy was!

Birdy insisted upon staying by our side during the whole ordeal. Her gentle purring only served as a reminder of the unconditional devotion and love our furry felines provide us. I couldn't have been more proud to be her "human" mom.

Quickly new materials were purchased and installed, making sure that all the wire connection terminal screws were tightly in place. We felt quite sure that we would never experience the problem again.

Birdy has since passed away. I truly believe that if it hadn't been for one curious little cat and her fascination with the world around her, our home might have succumbed to the devastation of a fire.

~Gail Sellers

Shut Up, Boycat!

*Cats are a mysterious kind of folk. There
is more passing in their minds
than we are aware of.*
~Sir Walter Scott

Boycat always had something to say about everything! Whether the subject was a startled lizard, a passing bike rider, the next-door neighbor's children, or his empty food dish, our gorgeous, loving Siamese made sure he let us know about it. And of course, we were always glad to listen. Or, at least, most of the time!

But as much as we enjoyed his exuberant cuddling, his playful antics with our three young boys, and his very serious efforts to guard his home and family against threatening butterflies—all the while keeping up his "cat-ter chatter"—we did look forward to having some quiet. At nine each evening we tucked in our three bubbly preschoolers, kissed them, and turned out the light. Peace at last—with Boycat staying with them as self-appointed babysitter.

That way my husband Don and I had a chance to clean up, chill out, unwind, and head to bed ourselves.

Then one night our peaceful sleep was shattered with a jump on our bed—and very loud meowing. Blinking, I turned on the light. "Boycat! What's the matter with you? Quiet down!"

Instead, he pawed at the covers and moaned, then meowed again, nonstop.

I was furious. Jumping out of bed, "Shut up, Boycat! Stop it!"

As I lunged for him, he leaped off the bed and ran out the bedroom door, still meowing at the top of his lungs. I jumped up and ran down the hall after him. Man, was I ready to teach that ornery cat a lesson!

That's when he ran into the boys' room and leaped straight up onto my son Chat's bed.

I turned on their light. Oh, no! Why did Chat look so strange?

Touching his forehead, my heart sank. He had a raging fever. And was barely breathing.

That's why Boycat was so loud. He knew one of his beloved playmates needed help—and needed it fast.

And Chat got it. After several hours in the emergency room, he finally returned home with antibiotics. Waiting for him at the front door was Boycat, meowing a loving welcome.

And we didn't care how loudly he did it!

~Bonnie Compton Hanson

Sugar Magnolia

Miracles are not contrary to nature, but only
contrary to what we know about nature.
~Saint Augustine

On Easter weekend 1997, my daughter Jessica was home from college. I had flown to Philadelphia to join my husband for a "dog and pony show" arranged by the company attempting to recruit him.

In the middle of my first night in Philly, we received a call from Jessica. She was frantic. An F3 tornado had struck Chattanooga. Our newly built home was destroyed. Our cat Sugar Magnolia was missing! We flew back to Chattanooga the next morning.

We had rescued her from a shelter as a kitten. My daughter named her Sugar Magnolia (from a song by the Grateful Dead). She grew into a magnificent cat—fluffy, long orange fur, golden eyes, and the best disposition ever. She graciously allowed us to live with her and she made our home a happier place.

The devastation of our home was total—everything ruined or blown away. Emotions ran high. We were thankful to be safe and that the storm had claimed no lives. But where was Sugar Magnolia? As pet lovers know, these critters become an integral part of families and we had lost a family member.

For three days we searched through the rubble. For some reason, the local and national media picked up our story and gave daily reports on our family and our search for our cat. On the fourth day, the bulldozers were scheduled to clear the land. That day, only Jessica went back to what we now called "The Site." We had not found Sugar Magnolia and feared all we might find was her body.

Later that same morning, as my husband and I watched *Oprah* in our hotel room, the program was interrupted by a news bulletin announcing, "Jessica has found Sugar Magnolia!" We were stunned and thrilled as we listened to how Jessica had found her just before the bulldozers started. She was alive and miraculously uninjured, having been buried three days under the rubble in an air pocket.

Sugar Magnolia became the celebrity of Chattanooga and lived happily with us for many years. We had lost her. We had found her, and although now, many years later, she has gone to Kitty Heaven, we will never forget her or stop loving her.

For me, the whole tornado experience was a jolting reminder and reinforcement of my basic philosophy of life: The glass is half full. To this day, I keep a picture of "The Site" in my living room as a daily reminder that "things" don't matter—only lives—even if animals.

~Janet E. Lord, Ph.D.

And Baby Makes Six

Kittens can happen to anyone.
~Paul Gallico

She strolled up the steps of our deck, her tiny yet powerful pink nose tracking the scent of salmon sizzling on the grill. Skinny as a rail, this far-from-finicky feline had no time for gracious invitations. She was on a mission to fill her empty belly.

"What a beautiful kitty," I whispered while stroking her coat, a patchwork of dirty white, gray, black and brown.

She slid her body along my leg, anxious to bond with the suspected source of the tantalizing smells that wafted through the air.

"Looks like trouble," my husband teased.

He's an animal lover too, but for him common sense usually wins over sentimentality.

"I know, but look how skinny the poor thing is," I said as I scooped her into my arms, cradling her like a baby against my chest.

Then something caught my eye: the telltale signs of a soon-to-be-nursing mother cat.

"Oh no, she's pregnant—look at her nipples!"

"You're kidding," my husband said as he placed the salmon on the table. "I guess we'd better get her a plate."

Our guest perked up in anticipation of the impending feast. With no time for manners, this hungry little hobo practically inhaled the little mound of salmon we'd placed in front of her. Afterwards, she stretched out on the warm wood of the deck, soaking up the sun while licking her paws clean.

"A kitty!" cheered my six-year-old son as he raced into the back yard just in time for dinner.

"Can we keep her?"

"I don't think Chelsea would be too keen on that idea," I said, referring to the reigning queen of our castle, a fat and happy feline with no desire to share the attention of her human subjects. The last time we introduced a potential playmate, she snarled and hissed and left a special "surprise" for me to clean up.

"And we don't need a house full of kittens," my always-practical husband pointed out.

"Kittens!" squealed my son, his eyes lighting up like Fourth of July fireworks. My husband rolled his eyes, obviously wishing he'd kept his mouth shut.

If this cat birthed her kittens outside, I thought, they would be feral and unadoptable—another sad statistic in the growing problem of homeless strays.

As the evening wore on, our diminutive dinner guest ate up our undivided attention. In the hustle and bustle of clearing the dinner dishes, she disappeared like a shadow into the night.

I hope she has a warm place to sleep, I prayed.

During the next few days, I learned that this wandering waif, dubbed Lucy by one neighbor, had dined and dashed at houses all along our street. I imagined her as a weary, cross-country traveler, stopping only to recharge and refuel at convenient truck stops along a dark and lonesome highway—and I worried about the future of her babies.

I guess it's in Mother Nature's hands, I told myself.

A week later, Lucy reappeared. Although a little rounder in the belly, the rest of her body was still much too thin for a pregnant mother.

"What if we keep her in the laundry room until she has the kittens?" I asked my husband. "Then we'll find them good homes."

A tall order I knew, even for an eternal optimist like me.

Surprisingly, my husband agreed. My son jumped for joy.

Quarantined in the laundry room, Lucy was safe and well fed; but she wasn't exactly content. Accustomed to roaming the streets, this free spirit was used to doing what she pleased. Now she found herself trapped by the unwelcome responsibility of impending motherhood.

Despite her objections, our makeshift maternity ward offered privacy, protection and plenty of space for her to stretch her legs while we waited for the big day to arrive.

Periodically, we let her roam the house when "her majesty" was fast asleep in the upstairs bedroom. During one of these adventures, Lucy became strangely fixated on my husband, meowing and pawing at him. He repeatedly shooed her away but she kept at it with a frantic, almost desperate look in her eyes.

The light bulb of female intuition switched on in my head.

"I bet the babies are coming!" I exclaimed and we rushed Lucy to her birthing suite: a laundry basket lined with old baby blankets.

"What's happening Mom?" my son asked, his eyes wide as her body contorted with contractions.

"She's giving birth, honey," I answered softly. "We need to be as calm and quiet as possible because this is a big job for her."

In a matter of minutes, Lucy squeezed out a motionless bundle of bloody fur—ugly yet amazing.

"What's that?" My son looked like he was about to lose his lunch.

"It's her baby," I said. "And I think there are more on the way."

Lucy licked each newborn until tufts of fuzzy, down-like fur appeared, then leaned into the next set of contractions without a sound. I stroked her softly, marveling at how calmly she performed one of the most daunting duties of motherhood.

"Is it a girl or boy?" my son asked, anxious to find out whether he had a new sister or brother.

"We'll have to wait and see," I said.

Exhausted after this maternal marathon, Lucy and her new family fell fast asleep.

The next day, the unsteady siblings—one girl and four boys—inched around on weak, wobbly legs in search of milk from mama's belly.

"Why can't they open their eyes?" my son asked.

I appreciated his eagerness, recalling the first time I gazed into my own baby boy's eyes as I held him in my arms.

The kittens seemed to double in size overnight, as did their curiosity. They explored every nook and cranny of the laundry room, clumping through their food dishes and digging feverishly in the litter box while dust clouds puffed into the air. They squeezed through narrow passages behind the washer and dryer, played hide-and-seek in a stack of paint trays, and wrestled in piles of dirty clothes. This once plain and practical space became a playground of endless fun and fascination for them.

Day after day, Lucy dutifully tended to her babies' needs. Then one afternoon, she made a break for it.

I spotted her from the kitchen window, a flash of fur sprinting across our back yard. It didn't surprise me: what mother hadn't fantasized about making a mad dash from reality? But I wasn't about to become a surrogate mother to five little felines.

I acted fast, running to the laundry room and gently holding one of the kittens up to the open window while he mewed frantically. Lucy stopped short then bounded back to comfort her crying baby.

A wanderer's soul is no match for fierce maternal instinct.

I soon found good homes for all five kittens—and for Lucy. My son cried when one adoptive mother chose his favorite, the one he'd hoped to keep as his own.

This feline family not only touched our hearts, but also taught us some important life lessons about giving to those in need—and about letting go.

~Margrita Colabuno

Family Counselor

Mirth is God's medicine. Everybody
ought to bathe in it.
~Henry Ward Beecher

The stress of working and raising our hyper four-year-old son, Trig, had put a strain on our marriage like nothing else could. Life had become a day in and day out feat until one day Trig came running into the house carrying a dose of sanity. "I caught a cat! I caught a cat!" Folded over Trig's palm like a rag doll was a tiny black, caramel, and white calico kitten all ruffled up. It had come from the field beside our house. My first thought was: Oh great, it's sickly. What has he gotten us into this time?

But, because Trig seemed so happy, Steve and I let him enjoy his discovery for a while before insisting he put the poor little thing down. But Trig would not have it! He carried that poor cat all evening with the lower part of her body swinging gently left and right. Unbelievably, the cat seemed to enjoy it.

We explained to him in no uncertain terms that when we got ready for bed, the cat would go outside. Tomorrow, he could keep her on two conditions: she would need a clean bill of health from the vet and she would be an outdoor pet. It was enough that we already had two dogs that demanded a lot of attention. We didn't need any more stress in our house.

So, when it got dark, Trig finally followed orders and went to the back yard to put the kitten down. But she refused to be left and followed him all around the house. He danced around her and she tried to trip him with every step. They had bonded. Trig said her name was Sammy and she was determined to stay inside.

Steve smiled for the first time in what felt like months and put his arm around me too. "Looks like we have ourselves a pet cat!"

A pet cat? How could that be? I had never had a cat. My parents didn't like cats. The only place I had ever even seen kitty litter or a litter box was on television commercials. So, prior to going to bed that night, some friends gave me a crash course on cat food, catnip, the kind of toys kittens like to play with, litter and litter boxes and how to house-train a kitten. We were embarking on a new, amazing adventure. I was reluctant until I realized what was happening. In an instant, Sammy had brought happiness back into our home.

I thought back to a time when a marriage counselor told Steve and me that in order for a couple to survive raising small children, they had to learn to laugh together. Sammy is the answer. She keeps us laughing constantly. We get more than enough entertainment just out of the various awkward places she decides to nap: in a cardboard box, inside the cupboard, inside the dryer, in the dish towel drawer, or on top of the new package of paper plates. My personal favorite was the day I found her sleeping face-first on an oven mitt.

This may sound crazy, but even the dogs seem happier. They wait patiently, letting her eat before they do and allowing her to walk in front of them when I let them out.

They adore Sammy and she, in turn, loves teasing them. They play with her roughly but carefully. If Sammy ventures outdoors, the dogs round her up by gently pushing her back towards me or towards the back door, similar to the way certain dog breeds herd cattle. They do not take their eyes off her for a second, as if to communicate that they do not want to go back to life without her.

Sammy has taught me to live in the moment. Computer time has become mom and cat quality time, and is no longer about efficiently writing a bestselling novel. Also, exercising is not something I rush through like I did before. Because if I'm not enjoying my workout session, Sammy immediately interrupts it by refusing to give me enough space on my mat—and laughter quickly ensues. These days it is more important to me to be around my family and Sammy's soothing purrs than it is to accomplish everything on my to-do list.

Steve is smitten too! Nothing makes him happier than to discover that Sammy has killed yet another pesky mouse. She becomes a tiny hero to my big, strong husband. Even though this is what cats do, Steve makes a big deal about it for days.

Adopting Sammy has done wonders for our family. Steve is always laughing and smiling. Trig is less hyper. My nineteen-year-old son, A.J., feels comforted by Sammy at night while the rest of the world is sleeping and he's juggling college and working the night shift.

I used to believe cats were dirty and useless. They couldn't fetch or swim in the lake. They weren't smart and they couldn't bond with their owners. Of course, my problem was I had never owned a cat!

Some would say a lonesome kitten roaming around a huge field discovered by a four-year-old little boy was just a coincidence. I choose to believe that God knew we needed a cat and knew Sammy was the one for us!

Up till now not a single one of us has ever seen another cat in that field. Why Sammy was there that particular day is a mystery. And every time she brings a smile to my face, I think about how lucky we are that an ordinary cat brought happiness back into our home.

~Melisa Kraft

Healing Hands

*If you would know a man, observe
how he treats a cat.*
~Robert Heinlein

The wipers beat against the driving rain, echoing the thump of my heart. I slowed as a wall of water splashed over the roof of my Jeep as it hit a deep puddle. I was trying to hurry and drive safely at the same time, which was only sort of working.

My husband had called me at work just as I was packing things up and preparing to shut down my computer. The stray pregnant cat that had been hanging around our property had given birth in the cold spring rain on an open hillside. Four of the kittens were alive; two didn't make it. He was in such a panic that the remaining kittens would die if not kept dry that he grabbed the four surviving ones and put them in a towel-lined laundry basket with a milk jug full of hot water. This move escalated the crisis because he couldn't catch their mother.

I told him I would be right home and bolted from the office to make the thirty-six-mile drive home. We had to catch the mother, a feral stray, so the kittens could nurse. I understood why he moved the newborn kittens inside, but I wasn't sure it was the best decision. The mother would have moved them, I reasoned, as my Jeep splashed through another enormous puddle.

On my way home, I met my husband at our veterinarian's office to purchase kitten formula, bottles and a catch and release cage. In the event we couldn't catch the mother, at least we could feed the kittens.

By the time I pulled into my driveway, the rain had slowed. I dashed inside to inspect the four orange kittens huddled around the warm jug. The vet had recommended this to my husband. The kittens would snuggle against it when they were cold and they would move away from it when they became too hot.

I threw on an old coat and went outside to try to catch the mother. The cold rain soaked all the way to my bones and I knew she had to be as miserable and scared as I was. We baited the cage with tuna, hoping the aroma would lure her. We found one of the lifeless kittens in a dry spot under the pine trees, but the mother cat kept running away.

After half an hour of pursuing her, I went inside to try to mix formula and get the bottles to work. The kittens had been born three hours ago and needed to eat. The bottles were just as frustrating to figure out as was trying to catch the mother.

We followed the directions and poked needle-sized holes in the nipples, but could not get the formula to drip out. We tried to make the hole wider using a thumbtack. I held one tender little orange kitten that refused to eat. I dribbled formula on its lips hoping it would lick it and give me a chance to slip the nipple into its mouth, but no luck.

I placed the kitten back in the basket and leaned against the wall. We couldn't do this. We couldn't feed the kittens or catch their mother. If the kittens weren't returned to her, they were all going to die. I decided that releasing them was their best chance.

Back upstairs my husband was peering out the window. The mother cat was standing on our covered porch with one of her limp kittens. We both stepped outside and she ran, leaving behind the tiny soaked mass of fur. My heart ached.

"Get rid of it," I told my husband, the harsh words surprising even me. I was done. We had managed to rescue thirteen felines in the eight years we had lived here. We lost this time.

He bent down and scooped up the kitten that was smaller than his hand. Peering closely at it, we took in its tiny whiskers, itty-bitty paws, folded ears and closed eyes. I reached out and touched the cold little body, swallowing hard against the lump in my throat.

"Get rid of it," I whispered.

My husband, still mesmerized by the kitten, placed his other hand on top of it. When he moved his hand the kitten's paw flexed.

"Did you see that? It's alive," he said and placed his hand on top again for a minute, then removed it. The paw moved every time he did this. I wasn't convinced, but looking into my husband's eyes I saw a man who was going to fight for this kitten's life.

The urgent race was back on! We dashed into the house and wrapped the kitten in a kitchen towel. I threw my adult cat's buckwheat bed warmer in the microwave. Once heated we placed the kitten on the bed warmer and the kitchen towel on top.

My husband instructed me to keep rubbing the kitten in a circular motion to get its blood circulating. He went back to preparing bottles. He remembered seeing on Animal Planet that if kittens are born too quickly, the mother doesn't have time to lick all of them to get their blood circulating.

I rubbed and rubbed, still not convinced we could save this little guy. Every now and then his paw would flex. As I rubbed, my thoughts drifted back to the mother cat outside. She was in a state. She was soaked and had given birth and her babies were swiftly taken away. Despite all that, she trusted us because she brought this baby to us.

The kitten moved its mouth.

"It's alive!" I nearly jumped out of my chair. My husband rushed to my side and took over kitten revival duties.

He covered the kitten with his hands. Pretty quickly, it was impossible to tell the kitten had ever been lifeless. It was very much awake and hungry.

I had given up, written the kitten off. But my husband never lost hope. With determination and a heart full of love for that tiny kitten, he used his healing hands to restore life. I didn't need another reason to love him, but there it was.

My spirits lifted. We could do this—we could

catch the mother cat and we did.

I fell into bed that night exhausted. Mom and babies were reunited and sleeping soundly in the laundry basket. And it turned out my husband's decision to rescue them was the best decision after all.

~Valerie D. Benko

Daycare

A good neighbor will babysit. A great
neighbor will babysit twins.
~Author Unknown

"Look, Mama. There's a white cat."
Mary pointed out a white shape against the dark green of the pinion pines in our front yard. An elegant white cat surveyed us with piercing green eyes.

"I wonder who she belongs to," I murmured. Mary went over to the tree and stood on tiptoe, her tiny bare feet quivering with effort to reach our guest.

As if she knew the child was gentle and kind, the cat tilted her head to let Mary scratch behind her ear. "Oh, Mama," she breathed. "I'm going to call her Snowflake."

Our tiny home was already bursting with two adults, three children, two dogs, two cats, and two fish. I glanced at the For Sale sign posted next to our driveway. On top of keeping everything neat and tidy for the unexpected calls from potential buyers, the idea of taking in another cat overwhelmed me.

"Please, Mama!" Beth jumped up and down beside her older sister, straining to reach the kitty, who knew to stay out of reach of the smaller girl.

"Who do you think she belongs to, Mom?" At nine, Jim took his job as older brother seriously.

"I don't know. She's too beautiful to be a stray or feral. She's not very old, but she's certainly not a kitten. Let's ask around the neighborhood."

"Then can we keep her?"

"We'll see."

Deep in my heart I suspected that someone from the city had abandoned the cat. An hour later, we trudged back up our driveway. "Mom, no one lost a white cat," Jim said.

"Kids, we can't bring another cat into the house."

"But we can feed her. Right?"

"Yes."

"Hurray!" The kids charged up the wooden steps of the deck.

"We're not keeping her!" I called to their disappearing backs.

A week later, I slipped out into the garden by the pond as dawn glowed. I sat by the dark and still water, pulled my sweater close against the chill of the summer morning air as I sipped my morning cup of Irish Breakfast tea.

"Mrrow."

I glanced up as Snowflake jumped down from the pine tree and ambled over to sit beside me, both of us watching the pink and orange reflection of the sky against the surface of the water. When I dipped my fingers into the water, the goldfish came to the surface, and immediately Snowflake was on the alert, eyes glued on the flashing orange shapes.

"Oh no you don't," I laughed, deflecting her paw as she moved to strike at the fish. "Those are my goldfish." She initially resisted, but then relaxed and curled up next to me. As I rubbed her she flopped onto her back, silently begging me to scratch her belly.

When I felt the small swellings, I knew Snowflake was pregnant. Just what I needed—a knocked-up teenager. While I wasn't ready to turn Snowflake into a housecat, well, not my housecat, I couldn't ignore a pregnant cat.

I purchased nourishing food for expectant mommies, and Snowflake rewarded us with her presence every time we were outdoors, sitting with me in the early mornings or following the kids as they played in the yard.

We created a safe place for her to sleep and ultimately have her kittens. Snowflake allowed my children to pick her up and place her in the new bed we'd provided. But as soon as we walked away, she'd hop out and head over to my strawberry bed, through the wire field fence to our neighbor's yard to where she had found a small space underneath one of their many sheds. Our neighbor had many piles of wood, lumber, sheds, and abandoned cars, which made good hiding places for small animals and an even better hunting ground for a determined cat like Snowflake.

As Snowflake became heavier and bulkier, she was content to just sit and watch my children play. One morning, she failed to appear and I worried that an owl or coyote had gotten her. But later Mary ran into the house, face glowing, and announced, "Snowflake had her kittens!"

"Where?"

"Under the shed next to the fence!" We all charged outside and raced to the fence line. Try as we might, we couldn't see far enough under the shed to spy the kittens, but we heard their tiny mewling sounds. For several days, we saw nothing of Snowflake, but continued to hear her kittens. I had hoped my kids could see the kittens as newborns, but I explained to them about Snowflake's determination to protect her little family.

About a week later, my kids and I sat on the porch hulling strawberries. I looked up to see what looked like Snowflake coming through the fence, hopping over the strawberry hills, heading our way. She had something in her mouth.

"Mom! Snowflake is bringing us a kitten!" Mary cried.

The skinny, dirty, bedraggled white cat carried a tiny black and white kitten in her mouth. Snowflake dropped it into my outstretched hand, turned away, trotted across the yard, and through the fence. She reappeared with another white bundle. Five times she came through the fence with one of her kittens held gently in her mouth.

Snowflake's appearance alarmed me. It had only been five days since we had seen her, but she looked awful. Her eyes were dull, and I noticed that her nictitating membranes were not fully retracting. Our new little mother was clearly exhausted. The last time she disappeared through the fence, she didn't reappear.

We stared down at the kittens curled together in a tight mass of black, white, and brown fur, and I suddenly realized that Snowflake had brought her brood to us to babysit. "Jim, go get a box. Mary, there's a towel under the sink in the bathroom." Beth and I stared in wonder at the tiny miracles in my lap. Beth gently stroked between the eyes of one tiny kitten who raised its head to her touch and began to purr.

The kittens nestled together in their box. About four hours later, just as I began to worry that she had left her still-blind kittens for me to raise, Snowflake reappeared. Her movements were more brisk and her eyes were brighter. She was still bedraggled, but she'd made an effort to groom herself.

Snowflake had taken a much-needed nap.

This set the pattern for the next few weeks. Every afternoon after lunch, Snowflake brought her kittens for us to babysit while she took a nap and had a bath. Before dinner, she retrieved her kittens, who had learned to follow her.

Knowing firsthand how tiring pregnancy and childrearing can be, I could only look at Snowflake with admiration. Who could resist such a cat? When time came to find homes for the kittens, we opened our home and our hearts to Snowflake and one of her daughters, both of whom visited the vet to prevent another unwanted teen pregnancy. A delightful addition to our family, Snowflake and her daughter gave us many years of pure love, but no more babysitting duty.

~Kathleen Birmingham

Meet Our Contributors

Valerie D. Benko writes from Pennsylvania when she's not busy rescuing and re-homing stray kittens and cats with her Dr. Dolittle husband. She is a frequent contributor to Chicken Soup for the Soul and has more than two dozen essays and short stories published in the U.S. and Canada. Visit her online at http://valeriebenko.weebly.com.

Kathleen Birmingham writes from Phoenix, AZ, where she lives with her husband, three children, dog, cats, and fish. Kathleen and her family have always chosen their pets from animals who needed rescuing, giving them their "forever homes," a solution that works well for both their rescued pets and Kathleen's family.

Margrita Colabuno is a single mom and full-time marketing-communications professional. She graduated *cum laude* from Hiram College with a bachelor's degree in Business Management. She enjoys designing and crafting jewelry, to wear and to share, and lives with her teenage son and sassy feline in Northeast Ohio.

Claire Fullerton is the author of the novel *A Portal in Time*. Her second novel, *Dancing to an Irish Reel*, will be published in early 2015. She is a three-time award-winning essayist, and a newspaper columnist.

Bonnie Compton Hanson, artist and speaker, is author of thirty-seven books for adults and children, plus hundreds of articles, stories, and poems (including thirty-four for Chicken Soup for the Soul). A former editor, she has taught at several universities and writing conferences—plus loves cats! Learn more at www.bonniecomptonhanson.com.

Newspaper columnist, retired teacher, counselor and psychologist, **Janet E. Lord** is the mother of one child and is from Illinois. The majority of Janet's professional life has been in the education arena. She currently focuses on writing children's books and a weekly newspaper column for families.

Alicia Penrod received her Bachelor of Science degree in Sociology from Brigham Young University-Idaho in 2004. She currently does accounting for an insurance company in Utah. Alicia enjoys running in competitive races with her husband as well as hiking with him and her four big dogs.

Gail Sellers enjoys writing animal, children's and

inspirational stories. She loves cats and enjoys relaxing at her cottage. E-mail her at gailsellers2011@gmail.com.

Melisa Kraft resides in Benton, KY, with her husband and two boys ages five and nineteen. She also has two stepsons, one grandson and one granddaughter on the way.

Austin Tamillo is an elementary school teacher in Northlake, IL. He resides with his beautiful wife Joy, his two amazing children, one pampered pooch, and four fabulous felines in Elgin, IL. His hobbies include writing, running, and cheering for his beloved Kansas City Royals.

Stephen Taylor is a writer and graphic artist. He lives in the San Francisco Bay area. He remains a devoted cat lover; he lives with his cat, Maxi; performs catsitting duties for various feline friends;

and continues to volunteer as a cat care partner at a local animal shelter.

Meet Amy Newmark

Amy Newmark is the bestselling author, editor-in-chief, and publisher of the *Chicken Soup for the Soul* book series. Since 2008, she has published 140 new books, most of them national bestsellers in the U.S. and Canada, more than doubling the number of Chicken Soup for the Soul titles in print today. She is also the author of *Simply Happy*, a crash course in Chicken Soup for the Soul advice and wisdom that is filled with easy-to-implement, practical tips for having a better life.

Amy is credited with revitalizing the Chicken Soup for the Soul brand, which has been a publishing industry phenomenon since the first book came out in 1993. By compiling inspirational and aspirational true stories curated from ordinary people who have had extraordinary experiences, Amy has kept the twenty-four-year-old Chicken Soup for the Soul brand fresh and relevant.

Amy graduated *magna cum laude* from Harvard University where she majored in Portuguese and minored in French. She then embarked on a three-decade career as a Wall Street analyst, a hedge fund manager, and a corporate executive in the technology field. She is a Chartered Financial Analyst.

Her return to literary pursuits was inevitable, as her honors thesis in college involved traveling throughout Brazil's impoverished northeast region, collecting stories from regular people. She is delighted to have come full circle in her writing career — from collecting stories "from the people" in Brazil as a twenty-year-old to, three decades later, collecting stories "from the people" for Chicken Soup for the Soul.

When Amy and her husband Bill, the CEO of Chicken Soup for the Soul, are not working, they are visiting their four grown children.

Follow Amy on Twitter @amynewmark. Listen to her free daily podcast, The Chicken Soup for the Soul Podcast, at www.chickensoup.podbean.com, or find it on iTunes, the Podcasts app on iPhone, or on your favorite podcast app on other devices.

Changing lives one story at a time ®
www.chickensoup.com